2x2 FLOWER

2x2 FLOWER

1x1 ROUND BRICK

1x1 PLATE WITH VERTICAL CLIP

1x1 TOOTH PLATE

1x1 HEADLIGHT BRICK

KU-414-185

2x2 CURVED BRICK

BAMBOO PLANT

1x1 ROUND PLATE

1x1 SLOPE

1x1 CONE

1x1 TOOTH PLATE

CLEAN CURVES
Curved pieces will help build models with rounded edges.

1x3x2 HALF ARCH

1x2 CURVED HALF ARCH

...GETATION DECORATION
...all pieces, such as flowers,
...nts or transparent plates,
...decorate simple builds
...a picture frame. (See
...wer Power, p.15)

LEGO® TECHNIC T-BAR

THINK ABOUT WHAT YOU WANT TO MAKE, SELECT YOUR BRICKS AND GET BUILDING!

1x3x2 CURVED HALF ARCH

2x2 ANGLED CORNER BRICK

...SMALL PLANT LEAVES

2x2 ROUND BRICK

1x3 CAR DOOR

2x2 BRICK WITH WHEEL ARCH

WIDE RIM, WIDE TIRE AND 2x2 AXLE PLATE WITH 1 PIN

2x2 ROUND PLATE

2x2 RADAR DISH

LEGO TECHNIC CROSS AXLE 4

1x2 HINGED BRICK AND 2x2 HINGED PLATE

SPECIAL PIECES
If you have an unusual piece in your collection, invent a model to include it in! This white girder (below) works well in a space-age display stand. (See Space Station Display, p.9)

2x2 ROUND BRICK

2x2 DOMED BRICK

CONNECTING PIECES
Pieces that have holes and extra studs are a great way to connect different sections of your model together – and provide places to attach decorative pieces.

4x4 ROUND PLATE

1x6 CURVED BAR WITH STUDS

4x4x2 CONE

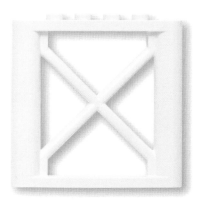

1x6x5 GIRDER

3

DESK ORGANISERS

Sort out your stationery with a LEGO® desk organiser! Before you start, think about what you want to keep in your desk organizer: Pens, rulers, rubbers? Do you need drawers? How big should it be? A desk organiser should be practical and sturdy, but it can also brighten up a workspace, so add decoration in your favourite theme or colour scheme!

BUILDING BRIEF
Objective: Make desk organisers
Use: Workspace organisation, decoration
Features: Drawers, shelves, dividers
Extras: Secret compartments

CASTLE DESK ORGANISER

This cool desk organiser has boxes for your pens and pencils, a drawer for smaller stationery – and it looks like a miniature castle! Start with the drawer and make sure it is big enough to fit whatever you want to store inside.

STEP-BY-STEP

After you've built the drawer, make a box that fits neatly around it. Once the box is high enough to cover the drawer, top it off with some plates, adding decoration and open boxes.

Layer plates, bricks, and tiles to build the drawer and the box it fits into

Need even more room for your stationery collection? Build boxes in various widths and heights

Simple, square open-topped boxes hold pencils and pens

Decorate your desk organiser with plates in contrasting colours

FRONT VIEW

Grey, white and black bricks are good for a castle theme, but you can use any colours you want!

You could use a large plate to build the bas the drawer, but sever small plates work if y reinforce them

Build a plate with handled bar into the drawer front so you can open it

EA MONSTER

are away stationery stealers with a sea monster
sk organiser! Begin with a basic box shape,
ild in dividers, then add the features that make
monster of the deep. Can you think of other
atures that could keep your stationery safe?
ve a go at making those, too!

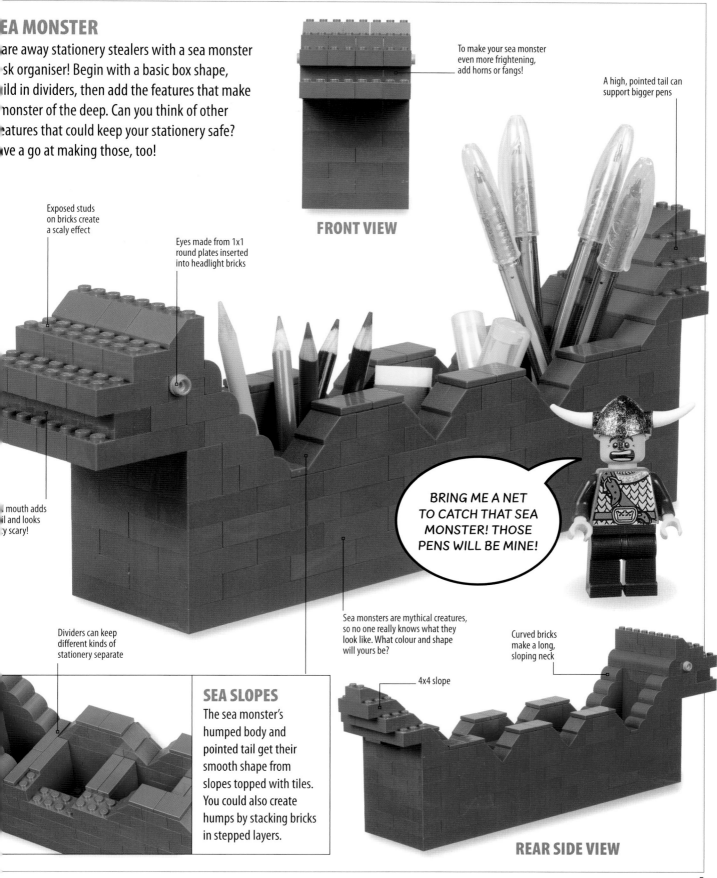

To make your sea monster
even more frightening,
add horns or fangs!

A high, pointed tail can
support bigger pens

FRONT VIEW

Exposed studs
on bricks create
a scaly effect

Eyes made from 1x1
round plates inserted
into headlight bricks

mouth adds
l and looks
y scary!

BRING ME A NET
TO CATCH THAT SEA
MONSTER! THOSE
PENS WILL BE MINE!

Dividers can keep
different kinds of
stationery separate

Sea monsters are mythical creatures,
so no one really knows what they
look like. What colour and shape
will yours be?

Curved bricks
make a long,
sloping neck

4x4 slope

SEA SLOPES

The sea monster's
humped body and
pointed tail get their
smooth shape from
slopes topped with tiles.
You could also create
humps by stacking bricks
in stepped layers.

REAR SIDE VIEW

TRUCK ORGANISER

Your desk organiser can look like anything you like. Why not take inspiration from everyday objects as with this colourful truck? It can deliver a truckload of stationery straight to your desk! What are your favourite things? What kind of shapes would make a good desk organiser? Try building one based on a car, an animal or a spaceship. Go ahead – it's your workspace!

Add lots of contrasting colours to brighten up your workspace!

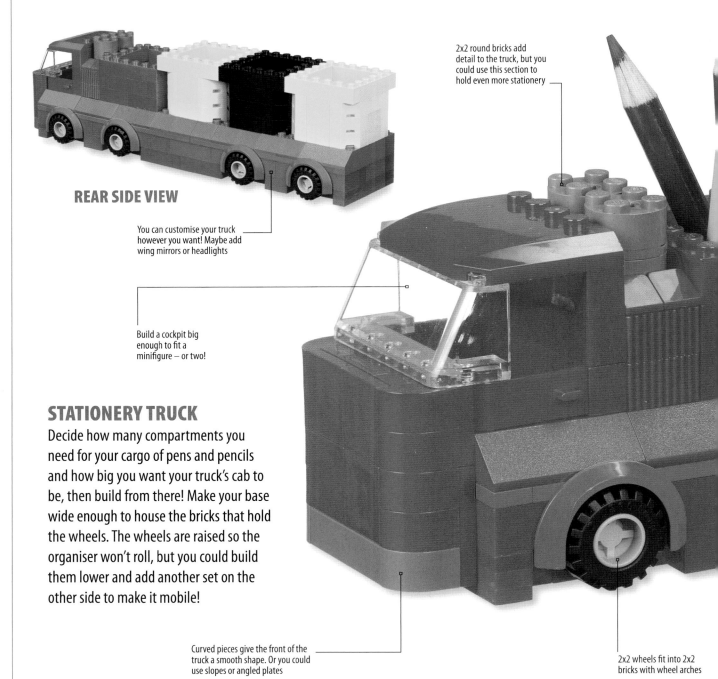

REAR SIDE VIEW

2x2 round bricks add detail to the truck, but you could use this section to hold even more stationery

You can customise your truck however you want! Maybe add wing mirrors or headlights

Build a cockpit big enough to fit a minifigure – or two!

STATIONERY TRUCK

Decide how many compartments you need for your cargo of pens and pencils and how big you want your truck's cab to be, then build from there! Make your base wide enough to house the bricks that hold the wheels. The wheels are raised so the organiser won't roll, but you could build them lower and add another set on the other side to make it mobile!

Curved pieces give the front of the truck a smooth shape. Or you could use slopes or angled plates

2x2 wheels fit into 2x2 bricks with wheel arches

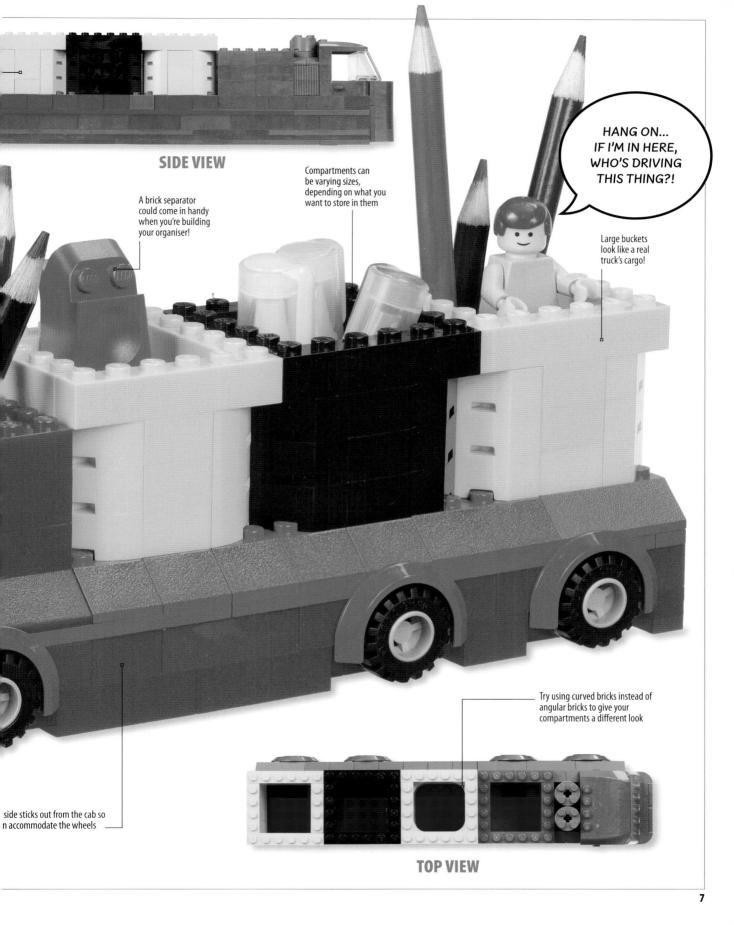

SIDE VIEW

A brick separator could come in handy when you're building your organiser!

Compartments can be varying sizes, depending on what you want to store in them

HANG ON... IF I'M IN HERE, WHO'S DRIVING THIS THING?!

Large buckets look like a real truck's cargo!

Try using curved bricks instead of angular bricks to give your compartments a different look

side sticks out from the cab so n accommodate the wheels

TOP VIEW

MINIFIGURE DISPLAY

Be proud of your minifigures! Show off your building skills by making a display stand to house your growing collection. You can add to your stand every time you get a new minifigure. You can even build stands in different styles to display minifigures from different LEGO themes!

BUILDING BRIEF
Objective: Build display stands
Use: Storage, decoration
Features: Sturdy enough to hold minifigures
Extras: Doors, moving parts

DISPLAY STAND

You can make a display stand with simple bricks and plates. Build a basic structure that is stable and balanced. Then use special or interesting bricks to add detail. Choose exciting colours, or maybe use a colour that matches your bedroom. It's up to you!

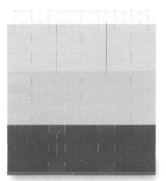

REAR VIEW

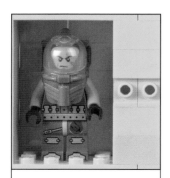

NEW HEIGHTS

A height of five bricks is tall enough to fit most minifigures nicely, but if yours has a large hat or helmet you may need to make the level higher.

You will know straight away if one of your figures is missing!

A mix of minifigures makes your display stand interesting to look at

Use pieces like curved half arc if you have the

Unusual shapes buil with half arches. Inverted slopes wou work, too

Use plates, tiles, so you figures can' fall off

Headlight bricks could hold tiles th correspond minifigures

NOW'S MY CHANCE TO MAKE A RUN FOR IT!

Accessorise to match the theme of your stand. Add antennas, some droids!

SPACE STATION DISPLAY

This space station stand is out of this world! White girders make this display stand look like something from outer space. If you decide to use fun and unusual bricks for your walls, make sure they're tall enough to house your minifigures!

Build the stand as wide as you need to contain all your minifigures

If you don't have a big enough plate, overlap smaller plates to whatever size you want

Could give minifigures a control panel or escape pod!

5...4...3...2...1... BLAST OFF! WHOA, WAIT FOR ME!

Girders come in a few LEGO® Town sets. Use any specialised bricks you have that fit your theme

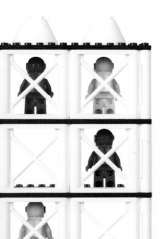

REAR VIEW

WORK IT OUT

How many minifigures do you want to display in your stand? Once you know, build each layer accordingly using pieces that fit your theme. These white girders look really space-age.

Choose colours to match your theme. For an underwater theme, use blue and green. What else can you think of?

If you don't have these pieces, try building with transparent bricks like windows – they look great as part of a space theme!

BOXES

Are your LEGO pieces all over the place? Pencils scattered over your desk? These boxes are the answer. Think about what you will put in your box and how big it should be. It will need to be strong and stable to hold all your treasures. Choose a simple colour scheme and design – or just go crazy with your imagination. Don't feel boxed in!

FRONT SIDE VIEW

SHINY BOX

This box will brighten up any desk – and make it tidy, too! The bottom is made of large plates, and the sides are built up with interlocking bricks and topped with tiles for a smooth finish. The lid is built as a wall that is slightly larger than the top of the box.

A row of shiny tiles finishes off the box lid

Choose your favourite colours for your box

You could increase the height of your box so you have more room inside

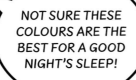

NOT SURE THESE COLOURS ARE THE BEST FOR A GOOD NIGHT'S SLEEP!

JOINTS THAT JOIN

The hinges are made from pairs of plates with bars and plates with horizontal clips. They are held in place by a row of tiles on top. To increase stability so you can use the box for longer, add more hinges.

Use curved pieces to make your box sleek

Bold colours will brighten up a dull desk

What are you going to keep in your drawer?

Build a plate with handled bar into the front of your drawer for easy access. Or you could use a different piece to personalise it even more!

Lid made from plates topped with tiles

1x2 bricks stop drawer from sliding in too far

Layer of tiles

COOL CURVES

Boxes don't need to be boxy – they can be curvy, too! Use curved pieces to create your desired shape. Make the drawer first, then build the box around it. Finally, create a base as a wall turned on its side. Use bricks with side studs to attach the base to the box.

Curved half arch

FRONT VIEW

SLIDING DRAWERS

To help the drawer slide easily, fix some tiles to the base of the box. These will create a smooth layer so the drawer won't catch on the studs as it slides in and out.

TREASURE CHEST

You can make boxes in all shapes and sizes – and to match any theme you like! Maybe you want a medieval wooden trunk with big metal locks to store your knight minifigures. Or a hi-tech, zero-gravity space capsule for your astronauts and aliens. Use different colours to style your box, and remember, the lid doesn't have to be flat!

BUILDING BRIEF
Objective: Create fantasy boxes
Use: Storage, play
Features: Hinged lid, drawers
Extras: Secret compartments, decorations

PIRATE TREASURE CHEST

This treasure chest has a secret drawer at the bottom for hiding your most precious LEGO pieces (or any other treasures)! First, the lower half is built around the sliding drawer. Then the top half is constructed on top of that, with a hinged lid, built sideways. The more hinges you use, the more stable the lid will be!

A layer of plates divides the secret drawer from the chest above it

Overlap bricks for stability

Press on this secret brick and the drawer will slide out the other side!

Use different colours to theme your box – brown and yellow look like a pirate's treasure chest

SIDE VIEW

12

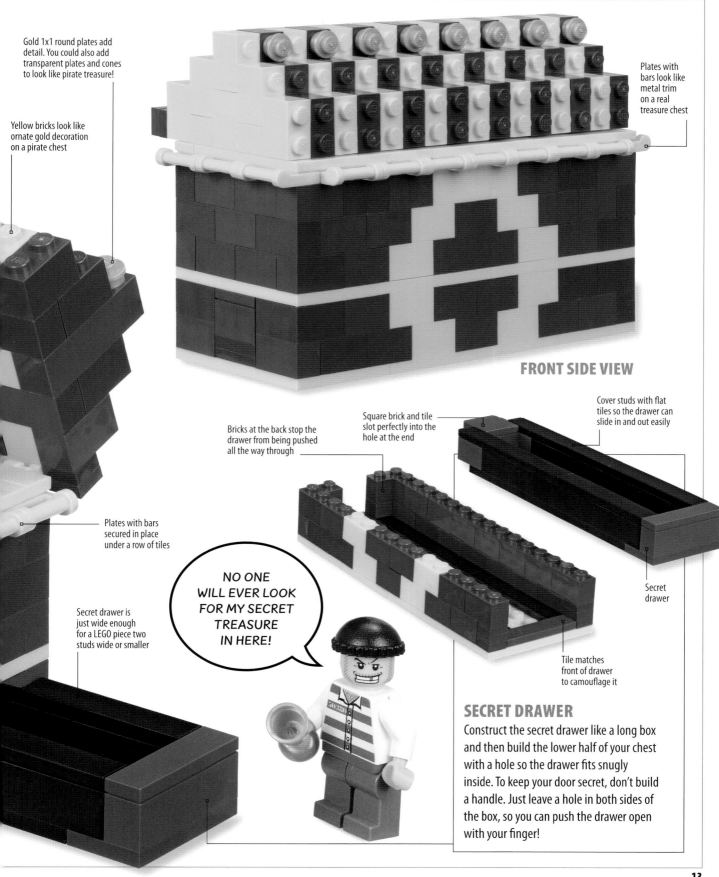

Gold 1x1 round plates add detail. You could also add transparent plates and cones to look like pirate treasure!

Yellow bricks look like ornate gold decoration on a pirate chest

Plates with bars look like metal trim on a real treasure chest

FRONT SIDE VIEW

Cover studs with flat tiles so the drawer can slide in and out easily

Square brick and tile slot perfectly into the hole at the end

Bricks at the back stop the drawer from being pushed all the way through

Plates with bars secured in place under a row of tiles

Secret drawer

Secret drawer is just wide enough for a LEGO piece two studs wide or smaller

NO ONE WILL EVER LOOK FOR MY SECRET TREASURE IN HERE!

Tile matches front of drawer to camouflage it

SECRET DRAWER

Construct the secret drawer like a long box and then build the lower half of your chest with a hole so the drawer fits snugly inside. To keep your door secret, don't build a handle. Just leave a hole in both sides of the box, so you can push the drawer open with your finger!

PICTURE FRAMES

Say cheese! How about building something to display your special pictures? You can use photos of your favourite LEGO models or treasured pictures of family and friends. Once you have a basic frame you can decorate it any way you want. You can even change the theme of your frame whenever you change the photo!

BUILDING BRIEF
Objective: Make frames for pictures
Use: Display your favorite pictures
Features: Sturdy frame, ability to stan
Extras: Multi-frames, themed frames, different shaped frames

BASIC FRAME

If you want your photo to be the main attraction, keep the frame simple. Use interlocking rows of plates to make two identical rectangles. A middle layer of one-stud-wide plates holds the two rectangles together and creates a gap to slide the photo in.

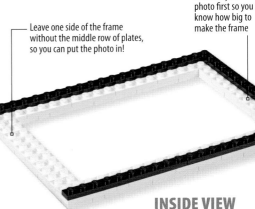

Measure your photo first so you know how big to make the frame

Leave one side of the frame without the middle row of plates, so you can put the photo in!

INSIDE VIEW

Add an angle plate to the top of the stand to make it more stable against the frame

Use a plate and a clip and bar hinge to build a stand

REAR SIDE VIEW

You could alternate the colours of the plates for a cool effect

SIDE VIEWS

I SURE MISS THE GANG FROM THE OLD NEIGHBOURHOOD!

FLOWER POWER

Now that you have the basic frame, you can get creative! Do you like flowers? Make them into a pattern to frame your pretty picture. You could also add some foliage or even a microbutterfly. Putting pieces at different angles creates an interesting pattern and helps fit more pieces on.

Use pieces that match your chosen theme

These radar dishes and transparent plates look really space-age

Use pretty flowers in your favourite colours

SPACE AGE

Why not decorate your frame to match your picture? This space frame has lots of translucent pieces and even a spaceman minifigure! To make the frame fit a portrait photo, simply move the position of the stands at the back of the frame.

Clip minifigures to bricks with side studs to add them to your frame!

Make extra pieces stick out to change the frame shape

Think of other pieces that would add to the jungle theme. Maybe a rope bridge or a mini waterfall?

JUNGLE FEVER

Add different coloured bricks to your frame to match your theme. Use brown pieces for a jungle theme and add lots of green foliage. You could even add animal figures. Go wild!

15

MOSAICS

Mosaics are the art of making pictures or patterns from small pieces of material, such as glass, stone... or LEGO bricks! First, plan how you want your mosaic to look. Will it lie flat or stand upright? Will it let through light? Will it be 3-D? You will have your own LEGO art gallery in no time!

BASEPLATE

A 16x16 baseplate supports these flag mosaics, but you can build your mosaic on any size base you like! You could also attach several plates together if you don't have the right size.

FUN FLAGS

Get patriotic and make your country's flag into a LEGO mosaic! These Union Jack designs are made from 1x1 bricks, with a few wider bricks where larger blocks of colour appear.

Use wider bricks for less detailed flags — it will save you some time!

Your flag doesn't have to be in the traditional colours — go colour crazy!

1x1 bricks help put lots of detail into your mosaic

1x1 and 1x2 bricks are stacked like a wall to make this simple design

FLOWER ART

Say it with LEGO flowers! This flower mosaic stands upright to look like two flowers growing against a clear blue sky. Tall slopes form a stable base to hold the mosaic up.

WIDER BASE

Toward the bottom of the mosaic, an extra layer of bricks is built into the design to provide extra support for the base. The ledge is only visible on the back.

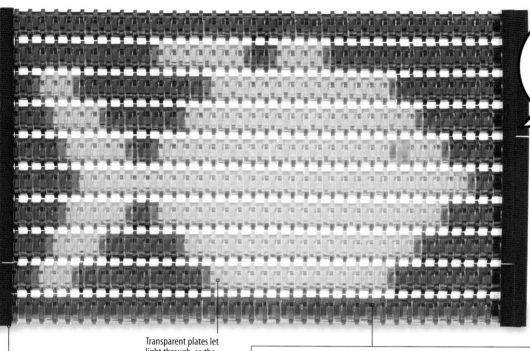

MARINE MOSAIC

This mosaic is entirely made from transparent 1x1 round plates. Ten rows have been carefully planned and assembled to make a floating yellow fish! Long black plates frame the rows.

Transparent plates let light through, so the mosaic seems to glow!

CONSTRUCTION

The design of this mosaic takes careful planning. Transparent plates are stacked according to the pattern, then the stacks are attached on their sides to the end plates.

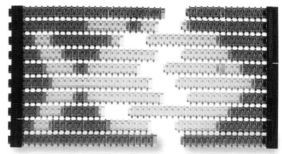

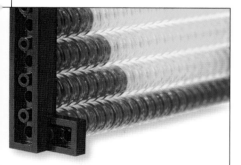

SUPPORT STAND

Add small plates at right angles to the end plate at both bottom corners. These allow the mosaic to stand up vertically, like a picture frame. If your mosaic is smaller, it will be even more stable.

ORANGE FISH

You don't have enough transparent round plates to make an entire mosaic, it doesn't matter. You can mix and match! This orange aquatic artwork includes white round plates, . You can include 1x1 square plates as well!

3-D MOSAICS

Mosaics don't always have to be flat. If you have bricks in different shapes and sizes, you could try adding 3-D elements to your LEGO mosaics to make them really stand out! First choose what picture you want to create, then decide which features will work best in 3-D. What do you want to draw the most attention to?

DID YOU REALLY HAVE TO DRAW EVEN MORE ATTENTION TO MY EARS?

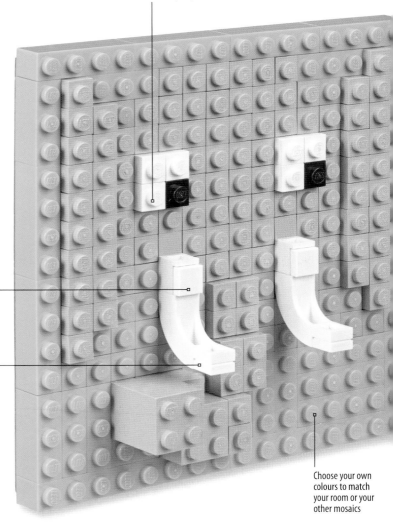

Layer bricks at different heights to add perspective

FRONT VIEW

White 1x1 tile covers the exposed stud on headlight brick

Choose your own colours to match your room or your other mosaics

TUSK TASK

The elephant's protruding tusks really bring the mosaic to life! They are made from curved half arches, which attach to the green background with white headlight bricks.

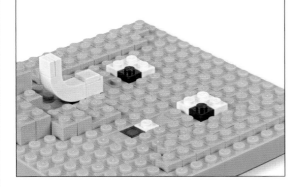

ELEPHANT

What is your favourite animal? Try making its likeness in 3-D! A 16x16 plate forms the base of this mosaic. The baseplate is completely covered in bricks, which form a green background and a basic grey elephant head shape. More bricks and plates are added to make the 3-D features.

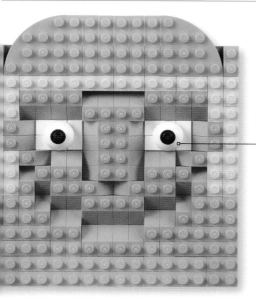

FRONT VIEW

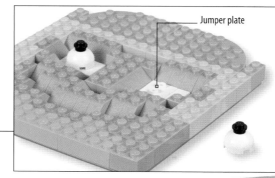

EYE-POPPING

You don't have to stick to square bricks for your mosaics! Here, the eyes are made from domed bricks and black round plates. The domed bricks attach to white jumper plates.

Jumper plate

FUNNY FACE

Don't restrict yourself to square bricks! Think about how you can form 3-D details with all different kinds of pieces. This girl's facial features are almost entirely formed from pink slopes! Used this way, the pieces create a cool, crazy-looking mosaic style.

Curved plates form the rounded sides of the girl's green hat

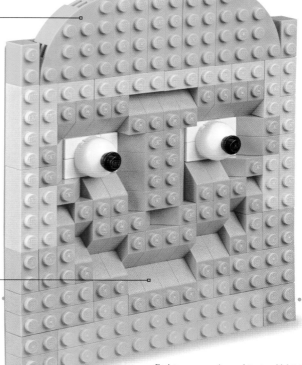

Arrange opposite-facing slopes to make smiling lips

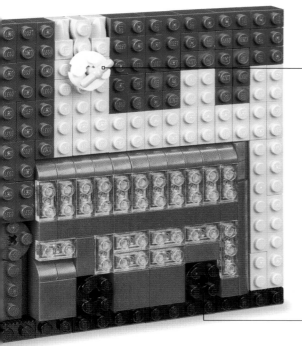

Big Ben's hands are a T-bar

CITYSCAPE

Lots of unusual bricks are used in this London cityscape. The clock tower, tree and red bus are all built using a variety of bricks. How inventive can you be?

Wheels are round plates

Clock tower built with tooth plates

Layer plates to add detail, like the transparent windows on this red bus

FRONT VIEW

CLASSIC BOARD GAMES

Classic board games can provide hours of fun. LEGO board games are no different – and they are ideal for long journeys because the pieces stay in place! All you need is a simple base and some game pieces. Don't know the rules? Ask your family or look online. You can even adapt the game to suit your favourite theme.

FINALLY, IT'S MY CHANCE TO CAPTURE THE KING!

Each side has eight pawns, two knights, two rooks, two bishops, one king and one queen

TOP VIEW

CHESS

A 16x16 base is a good size for lots of board games, including chess. If you don't have a baseplate, you can build one with overlapping plates to create a square. Then add eight rows of eight 2x2 plates in alternate colours to create a chessboard.

A standard chessboard has black and white squares, but you can use any colours you want!

CHECKMATE!

The chess pieces – pawns, knights, rooks, bishops, queens and kings – should be easy to distinguish. Will your queen have a big crown? Maybe your knight will have shining armour? Make sure the pieces are sturdy because they will be moved around a lot.

1x1 plate with vertical clip

Tooth plate for a horse's nose

Pawn

Bishop

Knight

King

Queen

Rook

Pawn

Bishop

Knight

King

Queen

Rook

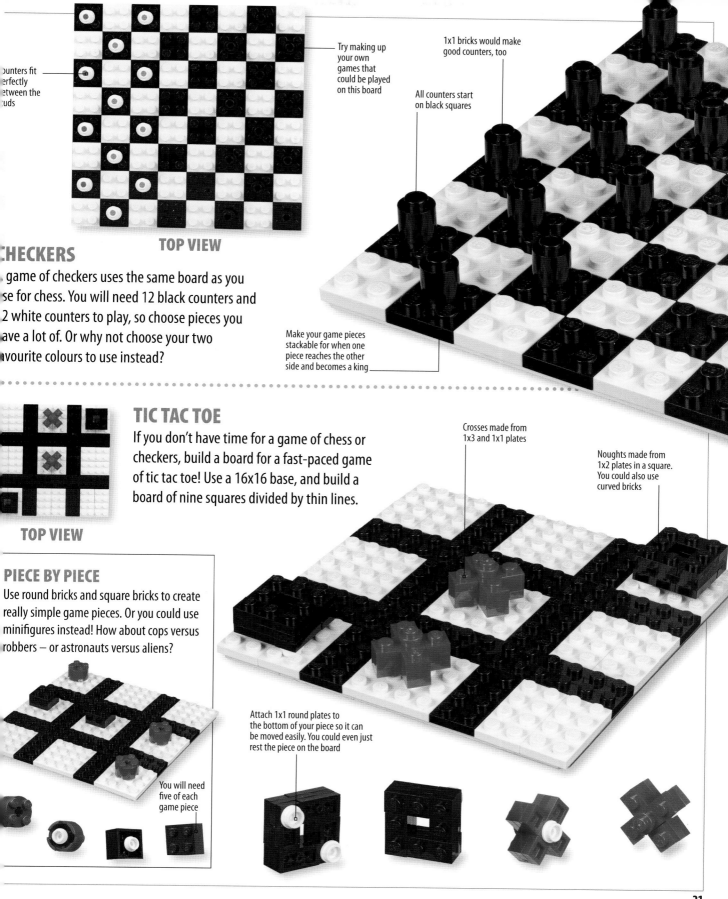

TOP VIEW

Counters fit perfectly between the studs

Try making up your own games that could be played on this board

1x1 bricks would make good counters, too

All counters start on black squares

CHECKERS

A game of checkers uses the same board as you use for chess. You will need 12 black counters and 12 white counters to play, so choose pieces you have a lot of. Or why not choose your two favourite colours to use instead?

Make your game pieces stackable for when one piece reaches the other side and becomes a king

TIC TAC TOE

If you don't have time for a game of chess or checkers, build a board for a fast-paced game of tic tac toe! Use a 16x16 base, and build a board of nine squares divided by thin lines.

Crosses made from 1x3 and 1x1 plates

Noughts made from 1x2 plates in a square. You could also use curved bricks

TOP VIEW

PIECE BY PIECE

Use round bricks and square bricks to create really simple game pieces. Or you could use minifigures instead! How about cops versus robbers – or astronauts versus aliens?

Attach 1x1 round plates to the bottom of your piece so it can be moved easily. You could even just rest the piece on the board

You will need five of each game piece

MORE BOARD GAMES

Now that you can build board games out of bricks, you and your friends will never be bored again! You can make all your favourite games, and even make up your own. Before you start building, try to organise the pieces you need. Think about how many people are going to play and what colours you want to use. You could even use your favourite minifigures as pieces.

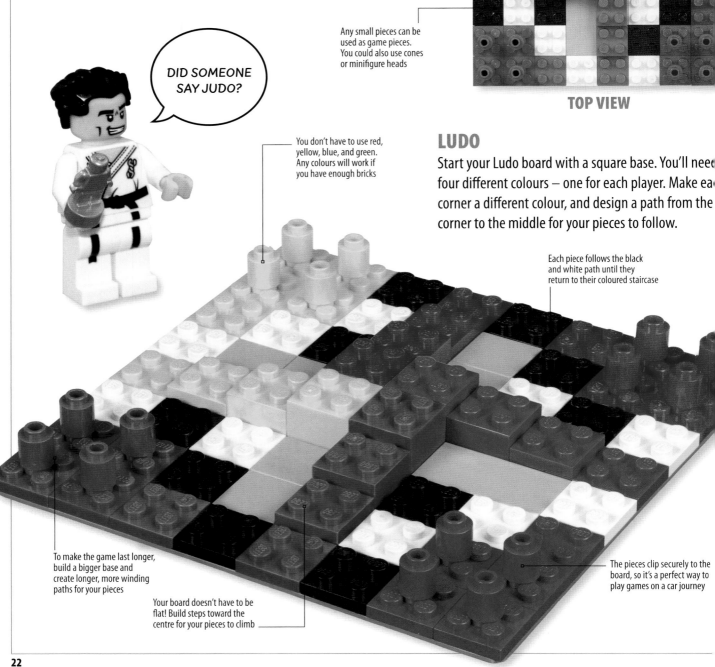

Any small pieces can be used as game pieces. You could also use cones or minifigure heads

TOP VIEW

DID SOMEONE SAY JUDO?

You don't have to use red, yellow, blue, and green. Any colours will work if you have enough bricks

LUDO

Start your Ludo board with a square base. You'll need four different colours – one for each player. Make each corner a different colour, and design a path from the corner to the middle for your pieces to follow.

Each piece follows the black and white path until they return to their coloured staircase

To make the game last longer, build a bigger base and create longer, more winding paths for your pieces

Your board doesn't have to be flat! Build steps toward the centre for your pieces to climb

The pieces clip securely to the board, so it's a perfect way to play games on a car journey

UMMIT

making up your own game. This one's called
mmit because the aim of the game is to reach
e top of the mountain. Build your board like a
iralling pyramid, with a path that gets a step
gher each time it goes round a corner.

COLOUR CRAZY

Choose one or two colours to use as the
default board. This model uses red and
white. Every so often, substitute a
different colour for a square on the board
to add rewards and pitfalls to the game.

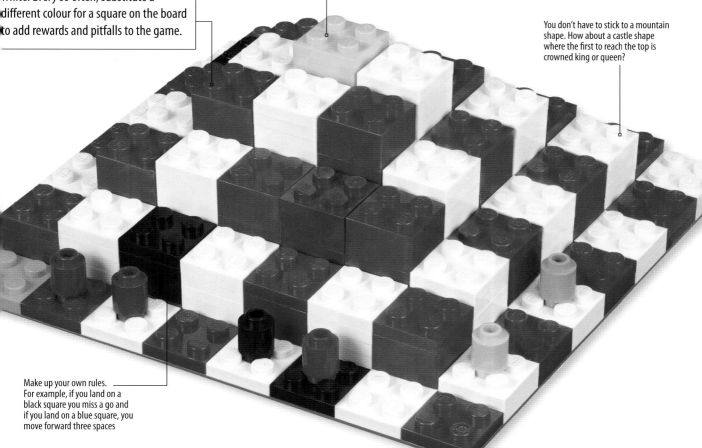

The winner is the
first to reach the
square at the top

TOP VIEW

You could place a flag or a
treasure piece at the summit

You don't have to stick to a mountain
shape. How about a castle shape
where the first to reach the top is
crowned king or queen?

Make up your own rules.
For example, if you land on a
black square you miss a go and
if you land on a blue square, you
move forward three spaces

BUILDING REALITY

You may have built lots of fantasy models to play with, from flying saucers to pirate ships. But now it's time to face reality! Recreating everyday household items is a different challenge, since you can pick up the real thing and take a good look before planning the best way to make it. Create life-sized models or minifigure-scale objects – it's up to you!

BUILDING BRIEF
Objective: Recreate household objects
Use: Decorative, storage
Features: Distinctive shapes, life-size
Extras: Ironing board, toaster

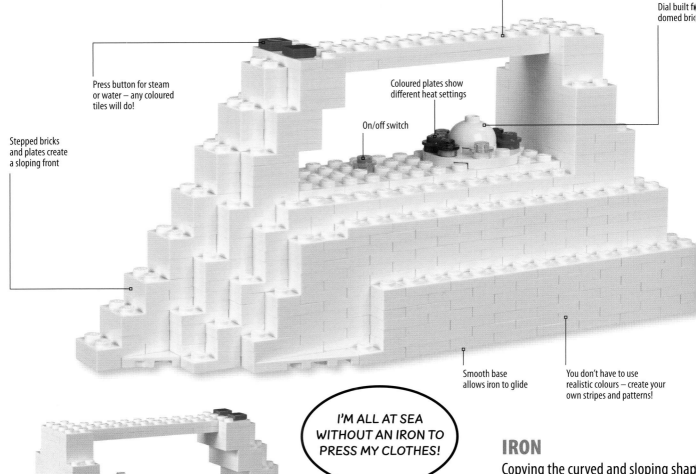

If you want to play with your iron, add more bricks or plates to the handle to make it more stable

Dial built f[...]
domed bri[...]

Press button for steam or water – any coloured tiles will do!

Coloured plates show different heat settings

On/off switch

Stepped bricks and plates create a sloping front

Smooth base allows iron to glide

You don't have to use realistic colours – create your own stripes and patterns!

I'M ALL AT SEA WITHOUT AN IRON TO PRESS MY CLOTHES!

IRON

Copying the curved and sloping shap[...] of an iron with LEGO pieces is a challenge, but it can be done! Add dials, lights and buttons to bring you[...] model to life – without the fear of burning your clothes! Just make sure[...] any real iron is turned off and unplugged before you touch it!

REAR SIDE VIEW

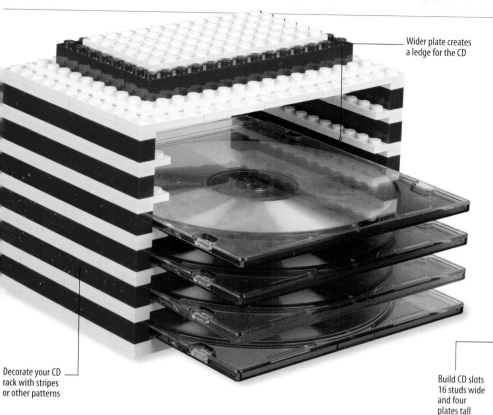

Wider plate creates a ledge for the CD

CD RACK

Sometimes LEGO builds are so realistic, they can function like the real thing! This CD rack is big and sturdy enough to hold your CD collection. Build two walls on opposite sides of a base, adding wider plates at regular intervals for your CDs to rest on.

Decorate your CD rack with stripes or other patterns

Build CD slots 16 studs wide and four plates tall

REAR SIDE VIEW

ALT AND PEPPER

hese shakers can be the beginning of your LEGO dining xperience. Try and recreate what might be on a dining table, om crockery to silverware, or even a candelabra!

Holes in the bricks mean that these models don't hold real-life salt and pepper!

Corner bricks surround a central column of two stacks of 1x1 bricks

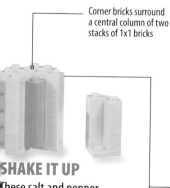

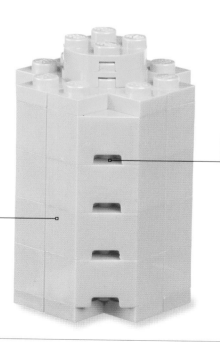

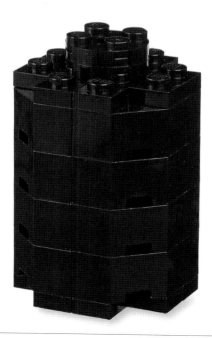

SHAKE IT UP

These salt and pepper hakers are made from ngled corner bricks, but ou could use curved bricks, quare bricks or curved half rches to create your own!

YOUR OWN DESIGNS

Now it's time to create some beautiful household objects using your own imagination! Instead of copying something directly, build a LEGO masterpiece of your own design. Use your favourite colours to build a decorative sculpture or think up original designs for a set of coasters that you can use – for cold drinks only!

Mixing round and rectangular bricks helps create a curve

BUILDING BRIEF

Objective: Create objects of your own design
Use: Decorative, storage
Features: Life-size, beautiful, functional, unusual shapes, fun patterns
Extras: Paper tray, placemats, jewellery

This sculpture is delicate. Can you think of a way to make it more stable?

Secure the round plates and cones with 1x2 bricks and plates

COLOURFUL SCULPTURE

Stack rows of round plates, rectangular plates, cones and bricks to make your sculpture as tall or short as you like. Choose your own colours and patterns to match the colour of the room you will display the sculpture in. You could even try building different shaped sculptures.

BACK TO BASICS

Build a circular base using plates covered with tiles. At four points around the edge, position 1x2 plates and jumper plates, to which you can attach the circular sides.

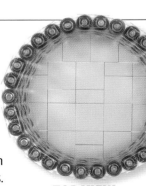

TOP VIEW

RCULAR COASTER

ur friends will be green with envy when they see s coaster! Build a round shape using bricks and plates in a single colour. Why not make a set to match your dining set?

Make sure the coaster is big enough to place your glass on

Start with a 1x2 plate. Increase the length of each row to the middle of your coaster, then start decreasing again!

TOP VIEW

Ten rows of bricks. You could add a row of tiles to the top so the studs aren't visible

row is 12 studs long, you can choose the to fit your glasses!

TOP VIEW

SQUARE COASTER

Stack bricks in a neat square to make this simple coaster. Decide whether to stick to one colour or go colour crazy and use as many as you like!

Print out or draw a rough sketch of your design before you start building

Start at the center and build your design outward

ON TARGET COASTER

Your coasters can be in the shape and colours of familiar symbols or logos, like this target coaster. You could even design a coaster with your initials in the centre!

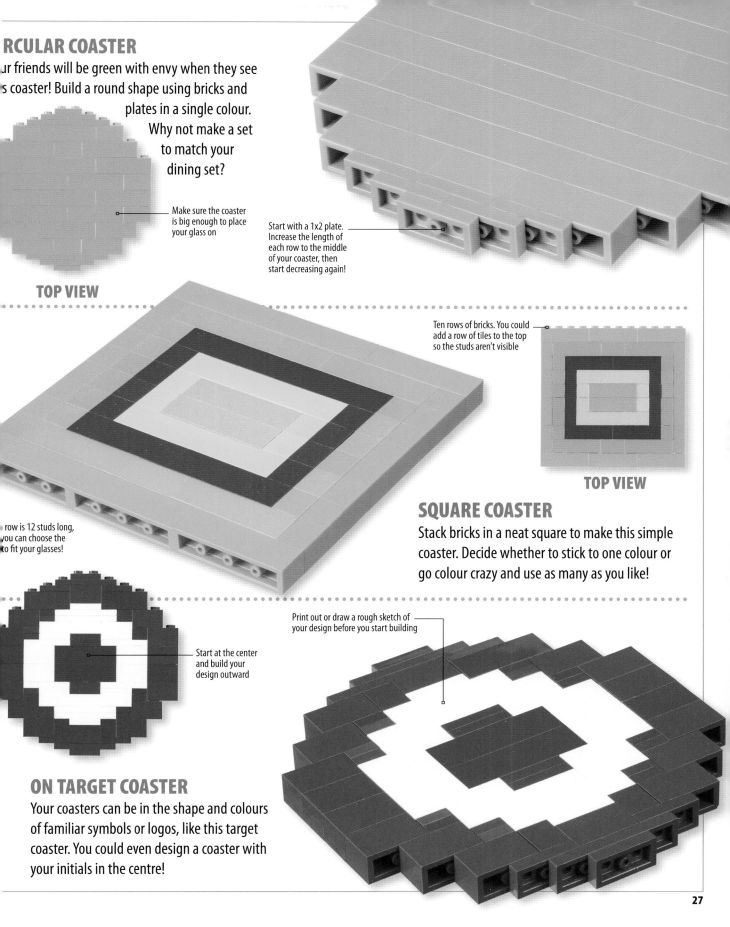

MEET THE BUILDER

ANDREW WALKER

Location: UK
Age: 45
LEGO Specialty: City, trains and still life

How old were you when you started using LEGO® bricks?

I'm pretty sure I always had LEGO® bricks to play with. I think they must have belonged to my older sisters and brothers. We kept them in an old baby bath, and I remember always rummaging around in it looking for the parts I needed to build. However, when I was 13 my brother sold all the family LEGO pieces so I was without it for many years. I have only started building again in the last five years.

This market stall sells LEGO pets. The little boy seems happy with his new pet snake!

This is a model of Stephenson's Rocket, one of the first steam trains. The most difficult part of the building process was mounting the barrel and getting the piston to work.

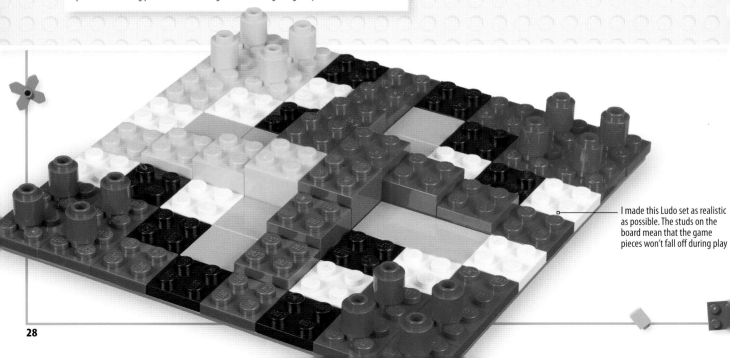

I made this Ludo set as realistic as possible. The studs on the board mean that the game pieces won't fall off during play

...hat are you inspired by?

...inspired most often by recreating memories, whether it's a
...n I've ridden on or a cinema I used to visit when I was young.
...o enjoy recreating scenes and models from films.

...at is the biggest or most
...mplex model you've made?

... of the great things about LEGO bricks is that you can build
...ether: I recently worked with five other LEGO enthusiasts at
...odel railway exhibition to build a train layout 6m (19ft 8in)
...e and 2m (6ft 6in) deep. We all brought our small individual
...els to build a lively and exciting town and railway. It looked
...t and all the visitors enjoyed our collaboration.

...e display, called Asteroid 478, was designed around many space vehicles. The command
...s solar panels, radar, communication dishes, sliding doors and its own repair robots.

...ou had all the LEGO bricks (and time!)
...the world, what would you build?

... of my favourite landmarks is the Eiffel Tower. I know the
...) Group has built an official model, but I would like to
...e one at minifigure scale with working lifts.

...at is your favourite creation?

...e made a model of the "Mole" tunnelling
...hine from *Thunderbirds*. I love how the body
...ogether and the LEGO bricks come together
...ake a round shape.

What things have gone wrong
and how have you dealt with them?

I have often built the body of a train only to find out that when I put
the wheels on it won't go round the track or connect to any of the
carriages or wagons! If you build your train too long it will overhang
and hit everything else as it goes round the corner, so you need to be
aware of the size and shape of your track. The wheels on trains are
also important – if attached in the wrong place the train will not be
able to travel around the track. To avoid this, always start with the
wheels and base of your model. Check how it goes around the track
and connects to the rest of your rolling stock, and then build the
body of your model.

This model of a classic car takes us into the future of personal transport.
It has a distinctive classic long nose and front grill, and I've added six
wheels, a bulbous cabin, smooth sides and curved trunk.

I really enjoyed
building somewhere
for my collectible
minifigures to stay.
It's great to display
your favourites!

What are some of your top LEGO building tips?

Try to keep up to date with new developments. The LEGO Group are continually bringing out new bricks, which really helps you when trying to build something from real life. Some of my favourite recent bricks include: the headlight brick, which enables other bricks to be connected in different ways and can help you build in close quarters; bricks with side studs, which revolutionise how we can build details into our models; and the 1x1 plate with side ring which enables the bottom of two bricks to be joined together.

Which model were you most proud of as a young LEGO builder?

When I was about seven years old, I won a town themed building competition in a local department store. I built a jail in a town scene and enjoyed spending the prize money on more LEGO bricks!

Building this underground rescue vehicle with drill presented some interesting challenges: using curved pieces to create a round body and using LEGO Technic beams to attach it to the base.

The hungry penguins are robbing the fish stall! Sometimes finding just the right minifigure head for your scene can be difficult, but this minifigure has the perfect expression!

The little figures on this clock tower are supposed to be like those that come out when the clock strikes the hour. When the LEGO Group released the trophies I knew what I had to make!

ONE OF THE GREAT THINGS ABOUT LEGO BRICKS IS THAT YOU CAN BUILD TOGETHER.

What else do you enjoy making, apart from practical makes?

Practical items are really amazing to make. I also enjoy building town scenes, with all the cars, trains, buildings and people needed to make an accurate mini model of real life.

What is your favourite LEGO building technique or technique you use the most?

In the AFOL (Adult Fans Of LEGO) forums we refer to SNOT (Studs Not On Top) – the ability to build shapes that are smooth, round and flat, without any studs showing. This is how I like to build.

How much time do you spend building?

I usually build for one or two hours a day, depending on what project I have on the go. Sometimes I might also have to do some sorting or tidying up.

How many LEGO bricks do you have?

I must have over 50,000 by now.

Do you plan out your build? If so, how?

Planning is often very helpful. I use the LEGO Group's Digital Designer virtual building software, which helps me go over designs and particular techniques until I am happy. I also use spreadsheets to help me plan out the number of bricks I need to buy. However, if I have to make something using only the bricks I have already then I just start building and use trial and error to work it out.

My creation of this iconic British train is one of my most recent builds. Getting the doors at the rear right were the final piece of the build.

ng parts from some of the LEGO Group's most recent sets I tried to reate my own car with a minifigure inside. With models like this, you y have to compromise or adapt to get your model to fit together.

What is your favourite EGO brick or piece?

think my favorite at the moment is the x1 slope that has been introduced over e last couple of years.

This treasure chest is the perfect place to hide all your favourite LEGO pieces! Building using specific colour design requires a little extra planning to make sure that the pieces colour coordinate but also fit together securely

Senior Editor Laura Gilbert
Editors Jo Casey, Hannah Dolan, Emma Grange, Shari Last, Catherine Saunders, Lisa Stock, Victoria Taylor, Natalie Edwards, Matt Jones, Helen Leech, Clare Millar, Rosie Peet
Senior Cover Designer Mark Penfound
Senior Designers Nathan Martin, David McDonald, Anthony Limerick
Designers Owen Bennett, Lynne Moulding, Robert Perry, Lisa Sodeau, Ron Stobbart, Rhys Thomas, Toby Truphet, Thelma Jane-Robb, Gema Salamanca, Abi Wright
Pre-Production Producer Kavita Varma
Senior Producer Kathleen McNally
Managing Editor Paula Regan
Design Managers Jo Connor, Guy Harvey
Creative Manager Sarah Harland
Publisher Julie Ferris
Art Director Lisa Lanzarini
Publishing Director Simon Beecroft

Photography by Gary Ombler,
Brian Poulsen and Tim Trøjborg

Acknowledgements
Dorling Kindersley would like to thank: Stephanie Lawrence, Randi Sørensen and Corinna van Delden at the LEGO Group; Sebastiaan Arts, Tim Goddard, Deborah Higdon, Barney Main, Duncan Titmarsh (www.bright-bricks.com) and Andrew Walker for their amazing models; Jeff van Winden for additional building; Daniel Lipkowitz for his fantastic text; Gary Ombler, Brian Poulsen and Tim Trøjborg for their brilliant photography; Rachel Peng and Bo Wei at IM Studios

This edition published in 2020
First published in Great Britain in 2017 by
Dorling Kindersley Limited, One Embassy Gardens,
8 Viaduct Gardens, London, SW11 7BW

Contains material previously published in
The LEGO® Ideas Book (2011)

001-322976-Jul/20
Page design copyright © 2020 Dorling Kindersley Limited.
A Penguin Random House Company.

LEGO, the LEGO logo, the Minifigure and the Brick and Knob configurations are trademarks of the LEGO Group. ©2020 The LEGO Group.
Manufactured by Dorling Kindersley, One Embassy Gardens, 8 Viaduct Gardens, London, SW11 7BW under licence from the LEGO Group.

Newport Library and
Information Service

All rights reserved.
Without limiting the rights under the copyright reserved above, no part of this publication may be reproduced, stored in, or introduced into a retrieval system, or transmitted, in any form, or by any means (electronic, mechanical, photocopying, recording, or otherwise), without the prior written permission of the copyright owner.

A CIP catalogue record for this book is available from the British Library.

ISBN: 978-0-24148-462-3

Printed in Slovakia

www.dk.com
www.LEGO.com

For the curious

PILL 21-01-21.